Anonymous

A practical method for the constitutional union of the

United Kingdom and the nine parliamentary colonies

Anonymous

A practical method for the constitutional union of the United Kingdom and the nine parliamentary colonies

ISBN/EAN: 9783337175511

Printed in Europe, USA, Canada, Australia, Japan

Cover: Foto ©ninafisch / pixelio.de

More available books at **www.hansebooks.com**

A

PRACTICAL METHOD

FOR THE

CONSTITUTIONAL UNION

OF THE

UNITED KINGDOM

AND THE

NINE PARLIAMENTARY COLONIES,

ON THE BASIS OF HISTORICAL PRECEDENTS; WITH
REMARKS ON A COMMON SYSTEM OF HOME
AND COLONIAL DEFENCE.

LONDON:
EDWARD STANFORD, 55, CHARING CROSS.

—

1880.

INTRODUCTORY.

PUBLIC opinion, on the part of Liberals and Conservatives alike, has been so emphatically declared in favour of a legislative union of the British parliamentary colonies with the mother country, that it has become no longer necessary to advocate the proposition merely in a general way. The question is now ripe for determining the actual method by which this union is to be effected.

A settlement of this importance must of course constitute a serious crisis in the national career. Like the union of England and Scotland in 1707, and the union of Great Britain and Ireland in 1800, the union of the United Kingdom with the nine British parliamentary colonies, calls for a decisive and lasting measure, one in which no sign of weakness can be discerned, while a vast accession of strength to the whole monarchy will be made manifest

Some timid folks, scared by their own half-conceived thoughts, have talked about meeting the claim for union by the appointment of a Council to advise Her Majesty's Secretary of State for the

Colonies. This idea is taken from the Council of experienced Indian officials attached to the Secretary of State for India. But those who suggest such a notion forget that British colonists who have won for themselves local Parliaments and responsible ministries, require a different treatment from conquered aliens who have yet to be formed into a nation, and have yet to be imbued as a people with the first conceptions of civil and religious liberty. In process of time the discordant races of India may learn, from English training and example, to become fitted for freedom and for participation in self-government; but it is impossible to place them at present on that political level, for which, on the contrary, British colonists have proved themselves to be eminently fitted.

No such lame and impotent conclusion as a colonial council, no halting or half-measure whatever, will satisfy full-grown colonial politicians, the representatives of men who have recovered our colonies from the waste, and have made them homes of British people, with laws and institutions springing from British instincts. Nor will it suit the parent country by whose arms those lands were won; by whose children they are occupied; and by whose power they are shielded. The nine parliamentary colonies must be made—in the words of an eminent colonist—" integral parts of one great whole "; and concerning the colonists, the same author insists that " it should be no bar to a man's promotion that he lived beyond the seas," as it is at present in respect of all the great national services.

The claim to the united exercise of full political rights, and to all the privileges thereof, inherent in our common brotherhood and nationality, none but a few mistaken (if not heartless) doctrinaires and false economists now presume either to deny or to treat with cold indifference; as if it were no matter whether the colonists and the colonies become divided from us or not. Blood relationship and family ties; identity of language and sentiment; the same wants and feelings, habits, and manners; bind together the Britons in the United Kingdom and the Britons in the nine colonies.

There is besides a growing mutuality of dependence and community of interests between the mother country and the colonies on most essential points. For while we clothe the colonists, they raise for us raw produce and food; and in the development of colonial cultivation must be restored the balance between the population of the monarchy and its food supplies, relieving us from that dependence on foreigners which now exists, and which, if not checked, is calculated to expose the country to famine prices, if not to actual famine. The difference between a people under one rule, and a part of the same race who have set up another flag, is no mere theory, but a matter of daily experience in our dealings with the United States, as will be proved further on. A recent attempt in the New York corn-market to stop the sale of grain in order to force up the price as far as possible, is a case in point.

A distinct proposition is made in the following pages for extending to the nine parliamentary colonies, hereafter specified, the same rank in the monarchy as the United Kingdom, with a full participation in its legislative functions and privileges. The proposal would place the ten British parliamentary divisions of the monarchy on a similar footing in regard to local affairs. It would relieve the pressure which has long made the existing Parliament of the United Kingdom quite unable to meet the increasing demands upon it; and it obviates all the difficulties that have hitherto rendered colonial representation in the Supreme Legislature impracticable.

To make the subject clear, and the argument complete, the following arrangement has been followed :—

1. A brief account is given of the present political organization of the whole of the British possessions.

2. Attention is then directed to the nine parliamentary colonies, and to their special claims to participate in the general legislation of the monarchy.

3. Two of these claims are particularly considered ; the first being based on the importance of the colonial trade to the employment of the people of the United Kingdom.

4. The next claim is derived from the mutual interests of the United Kingdom and the colonies in a common system of defence.

5. The proposed mode of union is explained.

6. A general scheme of national defence is proposed, in which the navy is regarded as answerable for the command of the seas; the local defence of the soil, both home and colonial, including resistance and attack on shore and afloat, against the landing of an enemy, is otherwise provided for. The development of the " Royal Marines " is suggested with a view to the transfer to that force of the construction and defence of all maritime forts and arsenals, besides its naval duties. Finally, it is proposed to liberate the Regular Army, as far as possible, from the charge of home defences, home duties, and the like, so as to make it always ready for the field in any part of the world in the highest military condition, and *prepared* to move with the greatest rapidity and at any moment, in fact an essentially offensive instrument, for the general protection of national interests.

The expression of these ideas, however inadequate, necessarily amounts to an appeal of an informal and indirect character, to the consideration of the constitutional authorities, trusting that the spirit which led to former unions will again prevail on this critical occasion.

THE BRITISH POSSESSIONS

THE NECESSITY

FOR

THE CONSTITUTIONAL UNION

OF THE

UNITED KINGDOM

AND THE

NINE PARLIAMENTARY COLONIES.

I.

A GENERAL VIEW OF THE COLONIES.

THE British colonies and possessions are distributed among all the great divisions of the land and water which cover the surface of the earth. In Europe, Asia, Africa, America, and Australasia; in the Atlantic, Pacific, Indian, Arctic, and Antarctic Oceans; in all climates, and among all the principal races of mankind, it has pleased Almighty God to permit the power and authority of the British Crown to be planted on its own soil and under its own flag. This vast and unprecedented exercise of sovereignty has been acquired, and is maintained, not from a mere lust of possession, not for the glorification of mere military or naval power, but chiefly in the pursuit and defence of lawful industry. It is unhappily the fact that wealth cannot be acquired and retained by nations or communities without a watchful discernment of the political, administrative, and social changes required by growth and progress, internal and external ; nor without the vigorous ability that is necessary to make those changes. The object now in view is to persuade all concerned of the urgent necessity for a great advance in the relations between one distinguished class of the British colonies and the mother country, for their mutual safety and advantage.

In consequence of different circumstances, such as the nature and extent of the population, and the purpose for which possession is maintained, there are three distinct classes of British colonies, besides other territories.*

The first class consists of those colonies in which British settlers, with other Europeans, form the bulk of the population, and have already obtained from the mother country the privilege in each case of a local Parliament, with a responsible ministry dependent on the prevailing opinion of the constituencies, as at home. These colonies are Canada, Newfoundland, the Cape Colony, New South Wales, Queensland, Victoria, South Australia, Tasmania, New Zealand.

Secondly, there are the colonies with representative legislatures and Crown executives. The Bahamas, Barbados, and Bermuda have a Governor

* A tabular view of the whole, with some statistics, appears at the end of this paper.

and Council appointed by the Crown with an elective assembly. In British Guiana, Grenada, Tobago, the Leeward Islands, Malta, Natal, Western Australia, each have a single legislative chamber, partly appointed by the Crown, and partly elected.

The third class includes the Crown colonies which are governed by officials under the control of Her Majesty's Secretary of State for the Colonies. In some of these, the laws are made by the Governor only, namely, Gibraltar, St. Helena, and Heligoland. In others, the Governor is assisted and controlled by a council appointed solely by the will of the Crown, namely, Ceylon, Mauritius, Hong Kong, Labuan, Trinidad, St. Lucia, Fiji. In the following Crown colonies the Governor's council is appointed by the Crown, subject to the regulations of some enactment, namely: Jamaica, Straits Settlements, Sierra Leone, Gambia, Gold Coast with Lagos, Falkland Islands, Honduras, St. Vincent.

II.

THE PRESENT POSITION OF THE NINE PARLIAMENTARY COLONIES.

With regard to internal local affairs, the nine colonies in the first class may be considered as being already on the same footing as the United Kingdom, if not indeed on a better one, if security can be thought of less importance than personal convenience and public outlay. But with regard even to local affairs when connected with foreign powers, and particularly with regard to the supreme questions of peace and war; foreign policy, diplomacy, and consular agencies; the defences of the monarchy, including the army and navy, garrisons, forts, arsenals, naval stations, and dockyards ; the honours, dignities, rewards, and employments springing from the Crown ; the public service generally ; foreign, home, and inter-colonial trade ; postal and telegraphic communication ; and various acts of legislature affecting the interests of the monarchy in general ;—in all such great national and fundamental subjects, the colonists of our own race, lineage, and language, living on British soil and under the British flag, remain to this day as if they were aliens.

This alienation is not only of the highly practical character indicated by the subjects which have been specified, it is also deeply felt by our colonial brethren ; and it may be said that the sentimental aspect of the question is not the least calculated to influence its settlement. The eminent Judge Haliburton, of Nova Scotia, so well and widely known as "Sam Slick," and for some time a member of the British House of Commons, insisted —that the invidious distinctions between British subjects at home and in the colonies, treated them as two distinct people. "Sam Slick" remarks—"The organization is wrong. They are two people, not one. It shouldn't be England and her colonies, but they should be integral parts of one great whole, all *counties* of Great Britain. . . .

It should be no more a bar to a man's promotion, as it is now, that he lived beyond the seas, than living the other side of the Channel. It should be our navy, our army, our nation. That's a great word, but the English (at home) keep it to themselves, and colonists have no nationality. They have no place, no station, no rank. . . . They are like our free niggers ; they are emancipated, but they haven't the same social position as the whites. The fetters are off, but the caste, as they call it in India, remains. *Colonists are the Pariahs of the Empire.*"

These bitter reflections have been repeated, substantiated, and amplified by other eminent writers, among whom may be mentioned Mr. Haliburton, a son of the judge, in a paper on the Pariahs of the Empire in 'St. James's Magazine' for July, 1874 ; Mr. Herman Merivale on Colonial Distinctions, in 'Fraser's Magazine,' and his lectures on Colonization and the Colonies ; Mr. C. W. Eddy in a paper read before the Social Science Congress at Glasgow in 1874 ; Letters, edited by Frederick Young, on Imperial Federation, 1876 ; Bousfield on the Government of the Empire, Stanford, 1877. From the latter writer is quoted an extract from a speech of the great orator and patriot Edmund Burke, who said : " My hold on the colonies is in the close affection which grows from common names, from kindred blood, from similar privileges, and equal protection. These are ties, which,

though light as air, are strong as links of iron.
Let the colonies always keep the idea of their civil
rights associated with your government; they will
cling and grapple to you, and no force under
heaven will be of power to tear them from their
allegiance." — *Speech in Parliament, March* 22,
1775. Had such counsels prevailed in England at
that time, the Congress of the United States of
America would have had no just cause to adopt
their Declaration of Independence on July the 4th,
1776; and thus the natural bond between Great
Britain and the chief of her great offspring might
have been maintained to this day, with results to
our material interests, which may be inferred from
the facts to be stated hereafter, not to speak of the
losses in blood and treasure that would have been
saved, besides the humiliation which we suffered
in vain. Let us find consolation in the assurance
that we live now in more enlightened times, especially in the enjoyment of facilities of communication
that none but the highest flights of human imagina-
tion formerly conceived; but which enable us to
realize practical intercourse with our relatives and
friends, even at the Antipodes, in a briefer space of
time than it took not long since to communicate
between large towns in this island.

On the present occasion it is proposed to invite
attention chiefly to two of the points that form
the basis of the claim for the union of the mother
country with the parliamentary colonies, for they

appear to be of themselves sufficient to decide upon
its necessity. These points embrace the subjects
of home trade and national defence, both at this
moment of urgent importance. A few words only
may be interposed to observe that, in giving prominence to home trade and national defence on
this occasion, there is no intention to undervalue
the importance to the colonies of having a voice
among the representatives of the nation on all the
important matters before mentioned. It may also
be added here, that it must be very obvious that
any cost which may be entailed upon the colonies
thereby would almost certainly be less, in union
with us, than the cost of setting up several sets of
distinct establishments, which would become a
necessary consequence of successful attempts to
perform the same work independently. There
can also be no doubt that as small separate states
they would be at the mercy of greater powers, and
occupy a very inferior position altogether. Since
the complete failure of Professor Goldwin Smith to
win public support for the idea which he has been
advocating since 1862, to wit, that the complete
separation of the colonies would be better for them
and for us, it may be considered scarcely necessary
to allude to that aspect of the question. The
decision is not likely to turn upon it, while the
points which have been selected for particular
notice, may be said to be of a thoroughly decisive
character.

Assuming that the discussion of home trade and national defence will prove that union between the mother country and her colonies is reasonably demanded, the next step will be to explain the necessity for a readjustment of our parliamentary system at home, for the purpose of combining it with the parliamentary systems of the other nine parts of the monarchy which have attained to that privilege, and also for the purpose of providing for more satisfactory attention in parliament to the local affairs of the United Kingdom.

III.

ON HOME, COLONIAL, AND FOREIGN TRADE.

The importance of cementing the union of the mother country with her colonies, from a commercial point of view, was demonstrated by Dr. Forbes Watson, from the Trade Returns. By a series of skilfully-drawn comparisons, he displayed the fact that the colonial trade of the United Kingdom is of far greater importance to the latter than the foreign trade, especially with reference to certain material characteristics which considerably enhance the value of the colonial trade beyond the tabulated amounts.

Dr. Watson's instructive paper is entitled "The Character of the Colonial and Indian Trade of England contrasted with her Foreign Trade." It was read before the Royal Colonial Institute in should be available, wherever the responsible authorities require them. Otherwise the monarchy may be attacked in detail, each locality in turn, while each waits with arms grounded till its turn comes; instead of all being at the command of the supreme authority, to oppose the common enemy, with the most advantage for every one concerned.

The following quotation from Captain Colomb is in answer to a very able colonial critic in the 'Sydney Morning Herald,' and also in reply to Mr. Forster, M.P. :—

"The 'Sydney Morning Herald '* says:—' We want— we require no standing army here. If England does her duty, this colony at least will do hers. Increased and stronger harbours and coast defences, and a gradual filling up of the ranks, will go far to protect all we hold dear. Besides, in these days of rapid communication, additional troops can be landed on any shore: there is always sufficient warning of impending danger to enable the Imperial Government to send assistance to the places most likely to need it. . . . It is argued that fragmentary self-reliant forces are of no use, for to be of any value they must be fitted to move from one attacked point to another. Now this strikes at the root of what may be called our system of domestic defence. New South Wales, for in-stance, should not, cannot indeed be asked to pour her defenders into Ceylon, or the West Indies, nor would she expect to be similarly assisted. The only movable troops are those of the Imperial army. They ought to be shifted from one threatened or assailed place to another, as the occasion demands. The self-reliant isolated armies of the "fragments" of the Empire will do yeoman's service on their own ground, and that is all that may be expected of

* 6th and 15th June, 1874.

them. That is the reason of their being, and that is the object of the movement which has met with such laudable success. . . . But we need not follow Captain Colomb further, unless it be to record another disagreement between us. He believes that any expense incurred in repairing "the state of the Imperial roads," ought to be shared by the colonies. We think not. We impose no burdens on the mother country for the maintenance of our safety ashore; and so long as we are integral portions of the Empire, we believe it is her duty to keep the roads in repair. Her honour and supremacy are dear to us all; but they concern herself first and principally. Our share of the obligations we willingly do, and to the statesmen of Great Britain we look for the rest. . . . Self-defence and self-reliance must be the watchwords, and each colony will do its duty if it provides a force sufficient to protect its own territory.'"

Captain Colomb submits the foregoing passages to special notice, as they are directly opposed to his views. He goes on to say,—

"They form a candid, fair, and straightforward expression of that colonial opinion which is adverse to the adoption of any Imperial scheme of defence, as will be presently seen. Those few brief but weighty words, extracted from two very lengthy and very able articles, very favourable in other respects, are deserving of most serious attention. They cover the whole ground of possible objections to acknowledging that any Imperial responsibility rests on any fragment of the Empire outside its own boundary, save and except that portion called the United Kingdom. The truth is, that while every portion of the Empire now happily recognizes fully and absolutely the necessity for defending it as one great whole, opinion as to responsibility, if not much divided, is at all events left utterly undefined. Before, however, proceeding further I will give two passages from that remarkable paper, ' Fallacies

of 'Federation,' which must be taken in conjunction with
what has been already quoted. 'It must be borne in
mind,' says Mr. Forster, 'that so long as any colonies
are British colonies the British Government is bound to
protect them, and would protect them in case of war
. . . . and Great Britain is also bound to bear, and could
not avoid bearing, the chief cost of such war.'"

Taking this last passage in connection with the
general statements of the address from which it is
extracted, Captain Colomb concludes—

"The chief cost means the whole cost, less only the
expense of such local and purely defensive works and
forces, colonies choose to create or maintain. Any colony
may or may not provide means of defence. The British
Government cannot, in an Imperial sense, compel it to do
so, nor exercise control over the constitution or distribution
of such local forces or means of defence,—if created,—
beyond colonial limits. The fact of a colony not adopting
of its own free discretion means of defence adequate to its
requirements, or to the best of its ability, simply increases
the responsibility of the British Government. The responsibility therefore of the Government at home in the
matter of defence becomes greater in exact proportion as
a sense of responsibility on the part of the colony
diminishes. The less a colony does, the more must the
United Kingdom do. Now this is not a matter merely
between an apathetic colony and the mother country, but
it affects every portion of the Empire, because the extra
war power necessary to put forward for the safety of that
colony is just so much deducted from the force available for
the protection of other Imperial fragments.

"There can be no doubt that 'so long as colonies are
British colonies, the British Government is bound to
protect them' to the very best of its ability; and there
can be no doubt also that 'self-defence and self-reliance

must be our watchwords.' The point is, however, are these watchwords to be used in an Imperial sense, binding all Englishmen under an Imperial standard which they combine to defend, or is each Englishman to have a little flag of his own, and hoist it where he sees fit, and try to defend it or not, as he feels inclined ?

"The question to be first settled is this : What is protection? What is defence ? It is really only chasing shadows to devise schemes for the protection of our colonies ; it is only a dreamer's fancy to arm for defence and to emblazon flags with 'Self-reliance,' if we are not clear what it is we have to protect, what it is we have to defend. Are we going to protect the unity of the Empire, or merely to prepare to save what we can out of a possible wreck ? Are the strong to defend themselves, and let the weak perish ? Are Englishmen behind 'increased and stronger harbours and coast defences' at Sydney to regard with complacency the capture of Fiji ; to hear without dismay of the seizure of King George's Sound ; or that the foe has established a base of operations at New Guinea, or in still more suitable positions on some of the neighbouring islands?" Captain Colomb feels certain that "the able writer of the article would in the presence of such contingencies be inclined to think that the honour, wealth, and supremacy of magnificent Sydney were concerned 'first and principally,' and that so long as Sydney could spare a single man or had a single shilling available to help to prevent such a catastrophe she would not have done her duty did she not spend that shilling and dispatch that man. It is rather fancied that the writer now so strongly in favour of rooting all military power of defence to the particular soil on which it is raised, would then fling away his able pen and carry a sword across the sea for the safety and honour of that Sydney he so dearly loves."

Captain Colomb says: "I do not ask for 'standing armies in the colonies.' I only submitted that the several parts of the Empire should come to a common understanding

as to the defence of the Imperial strategic points, such, for
example, as Fiji and King George's Sound; and in proportion to the extent to which their honour and wealth are
concerned in the security and efficiency of these positions,
so should they contribute in common with the mother
country to their maintenance and safety as Imperial
strongholds.

"If the colonies think it is wholly and solely the duty
of the people resident in the United Kingdom to provide
for the safe keeping of these Imperial keys, they should
insist that they do it; they should not allow measures
vital to their own safety to be so completely neglected.
There is no use concealing the fact that the British
Government, labouring under the pressure of home constituencies possessing all the power, cannot be reasonably
expected to move far in such a matter except supported by
counter-pressure from without. It is idle to forget that if
cavalry and field artillery be deducted from the strength of
the regular army—our only movable force—the number
remaining would not provide the strategic points of the
Empire with garrisons, much less furnish expeditionary
forces, which the colonies imagine we can at any moment
'throw on any shore.' The Imperial roads cannot be kept
open unless such places are secured independently of the
protection of the sea-going fleets, and therefore if the
mother country and her colonies do not come to some
common and really Imperial understanding as to how
these places are to be provided with sufficient garrisons,
adequate defences, and naval resources, a great war will
find our fleets helplessly watching their bases, while home
and colonial merchant ships are being chased over the
ocean like hares by 'Alabama' greyhounds. The injury to
commerce, the paralysis of trade thus caused will be the
'chief cost' of such a war. It will fall on the mother
country and her colonies, not regulated by our own
theory of responsibilities in matters of defence or warlike
preparation, but practically *pro rata* on each portion of

the Empire, according to its commerce and trade, the
stratcgical advantages its territory offers for seizure or
requisition, and its relative geographical position to the
quarter from which the opposing war power is launched.

"Whatever, therefore, may be a true or false theory of
responsibility in matters of our defence, war against us
will not be waged on any theory whatever; it will visibly
press upon, and be most felt by the interests most exposed
to attack, and leave us to settle our ' " Alabama " claims '
and our damages and accounts as best we can among
ourselves. It is hard to say, therefore, beforehand, on
what portion of the Empire the 'chief cost' will in the
end fall. If Fiji or King George's Sound were captured,
Australasia would feel it most; were Singapore or Hong
Kong taken, each part of the Empire would suffer in
proportion to its India and China trade; and so on. If
our squadrons are tied to these places because they are
not defended nor have adequate garrisons in war, the
water districts of which they are the centres would be left
without efficient protection, and similar results follow.

" 'If,' says the colonial writer, 'England does her duty,
this colony (New South Wales) at least will do hers. . . .
There is always sufficient warning to enable the Imperial
Government to send assistance to the places most likely
to need it.' Clearly, then, he considers it the duty of the
people living in the United Kingdom to send military
force to every place 'likely to need it.' If this be a
correct view, it is as well the whole Empire should know
England has not prepared to do so. While she now, as of
yore, expects 'every man to do his duty,' Englishmen in
the colonies rightly expect she will do hers. But the
very essence of the whole question lies not in the sentimental expression of a readiness either on the part of
England or the colonies to do their duty, but to distinctly
comprehend practically what are the duties to be done.
When Mr. Forster says, 'the mother country is bound to

protect her colonies,' let it be asked in what way? Is her responsibility unlimited? And are the colonies not bound to help? Does it extend not only to guarding all the trade lines of each particular colony, no matter in what direction they lie, but also all English homes and interests scattered over territories in the aggregate sixty times her size? Are colonies neither to furnish men nor money according to their means, to help the people of the United Kingdom to do so? In that case the signal of Trafalgar must be reversed so far as the colonies are concerned. *It must stand thus: England does not expect every man to do his duty, but every man expects England to do hers!!!*"

This part of the subject must now be left with the expression of a hope that those who desire to see the question of national defence more fully expounded, will consult the decisive papers of Captain Colomb. It should also be urged that this is not a mere matter of ratiocination, discussion, or simple indifference, it lies at the very foundation of our national existence, and it is a subject of that magnitude which may exceed the power of any government to act upon, unless it is supported by an intelligent, well-informed people. It is believed that all the interests concerned can only be secured by a thorough union.

V.

HOW TO EFFECT UNION.

The turning point of all debates of this great national character, the settlement of the questions—Who is to pay? and what is to be paid? leads us to the consideration of the union of the colonies with the mother country; and, after every one is satisfied of the pressing necessity and justice of the case, the method has to be fixed upon by which the desirable aim is to be fulfilled. This brings us to the touchstone and test of the matter. Those who have approached it, appear to be more ready to sacrifice principles than to alter existing institutions. There is a wholesome and generally commendable dread of organic changes.

But such was not the fashion of our forefathers in dealing with similar eventful periods in our history. When England became convinced of the necessity for union with Scotland, she did not hesitate to reconstruct her own venerable, historic, and purely English Parliament, so as to admit Scotch representatives in both Houses.

There was no hesitation in abolishing altogether the separate local Scottish legislature, and in depriving the greater number of the noble peers of that ancient realm of their parliamentary privileges. There was a great, vehement, and prolonged outcry in the north against the sacrifice of national independence. But every one must now see that the union of England and Scotland in 1707, was a measure fraught with incalculable benefits to all concerned.

In like manner, the Parliament of Englishmen and Scotchmen, led by William Pitt, resolved, in 1800, on the admission of Ireland to a participation in their proceedings; thus securing the intimate legislative union of the British Isles. Again a local legislature and an ancient peerage had to be sacrificed for the good of the commonwealth. If the same degree of success has not entirely followed from the union of Ireland which has attended our union with Scotland, the cause is not attributable, at least in these days, to any want of liberality, self sacrifice, justice, or benevolence on the English side.

If England thus opened its arms to Scotland and Ireland, it will not refuse to embrace the colonies; and we may be assured that a legislature which in the past has proved itself to be so amenable to circumstances, will not object to reasonable alterations of its own constitution, having for their end and aim, the full incorporation of her worthy offspring with the mother country, and the advancement of the power and dignity of the Crown.

Lord Dufferin said lately—

"I believe at this moment there is not a single man or woman in this country who will not recognize the right of those brave men who go forth to spread the laws, the liberties, the language of Great Britain in every quarter of the globe, to retain, so long as they may choose to value and to claim it, their birthright as English citizens; and so long as any colony chooses to recognize the supremacy of the Crown, and its civil and military obligations as an integral portion of the Empire, so long it may safely claim its right to share in the past glory and the future fortunes of Great Britain."—*Speech at the Reform Club, 22nd February,* 1879.

We may indeed permit ourselves to advance a step further and ask—Whether the exercise of birthright is so much a matter of choice as a matter of duty, of duty entailed not only upon the offspring but also on the parent; and imposing upon the latter especially the principal share in the management of the national family and its hereditary estate, fructified it is true by the enterprise and industry of the colonists, but originally gained, and ever since secured, by the power, the blood, and the treasure of the mother country.

The question remains—How is the union to be effected? In preparing to reply, let us dismiss at once, as weak and insufficient, the ideas of mere federation, or of a council attached to the Colonial Secretary of State, or, briefly, anything short of the legislative and executive union of all the parliamentary divisions of the monarchy, including the United Kingdom and the nine British parliamentary colonies.

In approaching this subject it must be borne in mind that the Parliaments of the nine colonies only legislate for their respective constituencies, and are thus Parliaments for local affairs only. But the Parliament of the United Kingdom undertakes not only the local legislation of the three kingdoms, but it also legislates for the whole monarchy, besides discussing and controlling the relations of the Crown with foreign powers. So far, however, is the Parliament of the United Kingdom from accomplishing in a satisfactory manner the herculean task which has grown upon it, its admitted failure to do so has for a long time stood in the way of every proposal that has taken it as a basis for giving the colonies a representative voice in the national councils.

Now, therefore, a proposition is made, which has the following objects.

Firstly, To place the Parliaments of the colonies and the United Kingdom on the same footing, by limiting the legislation of the latter to the local affairs of the three kingdoms. By this means it may be fairly anticipated that time will be gained for paying that attention to home legislation, which has been notoriously long wanted.

Secondly, To constitute a Supreme Parliament of two chambers for the general affairs of the whole monarchy, in which the nine parliamentary colonies, as well as the United Kingdom, shall be represented proportionably. Perhaps also seats may be granted to certain other important colonial possessions, in which executive responsibility to the local constituencies has not yet been fully developed. But it is a question that may well be left to the deliberation of the future Supreme Parliament.

This proposed Supreme Parliament of the whole nation at home and abroad, would correspond to the Senate and House of Representatives of the United States, while the local Parliaments would be in the position of the separate state legislatures of that republic. Lest this comparison should savour too much of republicanism, another parallel case may be found in the present German empire, which has—besides its Imperial Council and Diet—local legislatures in each of the monarchies, principalities, and free cities which form the empire. Such eminent precedents may be fairly regarded as sufficiently apt and worthy instances of the method proposed for uniting distinct members of the same great nationality.

The subjects that might be withdrawn from the present Parliament of the United Kingdom and placed under the control of the Supreme Parliament, may be expected to include :—

1. Revenues and expenditure for extra local purposes.

2. The defensive forces of the monarchy as a whole.

3. Intercolonial, home, and foreign trade.

4. External and foreign communications, postal, telegraphic, &c.

5. External and foreign affairs generally.

6. Coinage, currency, moneys of account, weights and measures.

7. External and maritime judicial affairs and courts of appeal.

8. Naturalization.

9. National lands.

10. General census

11. National and other public debts.

The great changes in the constitution of the legislature of the United Kingdom which took place in 1707, 1800, and 1832, are a convincing proof that the three estates of the realm are not mere bigoted adherents to existing conditions when reasonable alterations are required. In a matter of the broad and cosmopolitan character involved in the consideration of British interests all over the world, embracing about a half of North America, a large part of South Africa, the whole of Australia, and numerous islands in all directions, it may be more difficult to impress the public with an adequate conception of the subject; so as to enable the nation to afford to ministers of State and members of Parliament at home and in the colonies, the support that a government requires which depends on popular opinion. The present proposal has the recommendation of being far less sweeping in its treatment of existing conditions than the changes which have been already undergone. On this occasion we are not proposing to do away with the separate existence of ancient legislatures of states as old as England, like those of Scotland and Ireland, nor to deprive any portion of the Peers of Parliament of their seats in the House of Lords. We do propose to give the Houses of Lords and Commons more ample opportunity to provide for the urgent and rapidly expanding claims of the local affairs of the United Kingdom, which are now agreed on all hands, and

by all parties, to be very insufficiently attended to.
If distinct Parliaments for local affairs are good for
nine parts of the same people, they may fairly
claim a title to consideration in other cases, and
they cannot be regarded as intrinsically objectionable. The present proposal does not necessarily
involve the revival of the separate legislatures for
the three kingdoms, although some may be disposed to believe that the time has arrived for
restoring the ancient Parliaments of Scotland and
Ireland, *so far as their local affairs are concerned.*
The absolute, indefeasible, and fundamental union
of the three kingdoms, or more correctly of the
United Kingdom, will be more effectually and
more emphatically provided for in a Supreme
Parliament, in which the British Isles and British
colonies will have a complete representative amalgamation, for the express purpose of concurrence
in the common affairs of the whole monarchy. In
alluding to this point, one feels bound to express
the belief that every candid person must admit
the immeasurable advantages which have arisen
from the successive Acts of Union. The united
legislature has brought English, Scotch, and Irish
into close personal contact on the same platform,
day after day and year after year, for the discussion of their united interests, and the elimination
of points of difference, so as to arrive at common
agreements, as far, at least, as the majority is
at first concerned, and including everyone after-

wards, in obedience to law. Such a school and
such a political discipline cannot fail to have had
most potent influences in drawing candid and well-
disposed minds to regard each other with benevolence, and to work in harmony for the common
cause; although we have seen in these present
days a few melancholy examples of wilful and
malicious obstructiveness. If the present question
implied or made possible the abandonment of such
a common platform and existent union, the writer
would be the last to propose it. No! our national
object must be, not to break up the union, but, on
the contrary, so to extend it as to embrace all
British people on British soil, our brave and loyal
brethren in the British colonies, as well as in the
British Isles.

For that great, grave, and beneficent purpose,
the limitation of the present Houses of Lords and
Commons to the local affairs of the United Kingdom is amply sufficient, without resorting to other
changes. But if it should be found hereafter that
the local affairs of the British Isles call for the
revival of the ancient legislatures, it must be
candidly remembered that, after a prolonged period
of legislative union, England, Scotland, and Ireland still remain separate in their laws, prevailing
religions, and local institutions. And it cannot be
questioned that the establishment of a Supreme
Parliament, exercising a common control over all,
and in which the British Isles and British colonies

would be proportionately represented, would go far to remove the serious objections to which such a measure would be otherwise exposed. This matter could hardly fail to arise in connection with the present subject, but it has been shown that it is not a necessary part of it, and that is the only reason for alluding to it.

Some of the details involved in the constitution of a Supreme British Parliament are of a nature to invite notice, even in an introductory discourse. All the details are of a kind that have had to be arranged in the two great examples presented by the United States and the German Empire, as well as in the amalgamation of the United Kingdom, and also in the recent case of the Dominion of Canada. They are therefore not of a kind to present any insuperable difficulties.

In the constitution of both Houses of the Supreme Parliament, it appears that a smaller number of members than that of the present Houses of Parliament is desirable. If the numbers of the present Houses of Lords and Commons be taken as a basis, it will be found that Canada would be entitled to 75 members in the Commons, and 15 in the Lords, according to the ratio of population. It may be supposed that rateable value ought to be an element in this proportion ; but in fact it has been shown by parliamentary inquiry that there is no adequate occasion to complicate the problem on that account, as it does not materially affect the result. The

1878, and is published by W. H. Allen and Co., of Waterloo Place. To reproduce his evidence and arguments thoroughly would involve the entire work. On this occasion we must be content with extracts, and an analysis of its most salient points; and as it has been contended that our colonial trade would be the same whether the colonies were united or separated from us, it may be well to begin by ascertaining what the trade returns state with regard to the colonies which remain united with us, on the one hand, and the colonies which have become separated from us (that is, the United States of North America) on the other. .

In 1876, the British exports to Australia exceeded those to the United States, although the population of the States is *twentyfold* greater than that of Australia. In that year, the exports to Australia amounted to 17,700,000*l*. in value, while to the States they only amounted to 16,100,000*l*.

Between the years 1869 and 1876, the exports of British home produce to the British possessions increased by 17,000,000*l*., while the exports to foreign countries diminished by 6,000,000*l*. Thus, but for the expansion of the colonial and Indian markets, the export trade of 1876 would have shown a diminution as compared with 1869; instead of which there was an increase in the sum total of exports from 189,000,000*l*. to about 200,000,000*l*.

Articles of dress and domestic consumption, while decreasing as exports to foreign countries, are remarkably on the increase as exports to the British possessions; and it is noticed that in the preparation of such articles, British labour only is employed.

Again, in the cotton trade, while there was only an increase of 3·6 per cent. between the years 1869 and 1876, that sum was made up by a decrease of 11·9 per cent. on exports to foreign countries, and an increase of 40·3 per cent. on exports to British possessions.

The silk manufactures show only a slight increase in the exports to foreign countries, while the exports to British possessions have become more than fourfold in the same time, having risen from 180,000*l.* to 818,000*l.*

In fact the same results in favour of colonial trade are found in every class of British exports, in proof of which Dr. Watson supplies a specific statement.

Dr. Watson distinguishes the export trade to British possessions by two marked characteristics. The first is the steadiness and rapidity of its growth, as compared with the violent fluctuations to which the foreign trade is liable. The second is the preponderance in colonial exports of *finished* manufactures, over those in various stages of preparation. The finished manufactures, of course, represent a larger proportion of British labour

employed upon them. It is inferred that more
than a third of the working population of the
United Kingdom is employed in that trade!!!

The fluctuations of foreign trade, and its charac-
teristic demand for partially manufactured goods,
are considered to be due to the fact that our supplies
to foreign countries are only subsidiary to their
own local supplies, and are adapted by the foreign
manufacturers to suit their market.

In the colonies, the consumers are the bulk of
the population, with tastes like our own, and the
trade is regulated by the growth of their numbers
and wealth. In foreign countries, our articles, to
a large extent, are imported by manufacturers to
supplement their own productions, and to be
finished by themselves, the extent of the demand
fluctuating with various circumstances, not dependent on the consuming power of the country,
as in the colonies.

The colonies, indeed, may be regarded as ex-
tensions of the home markets, the demand from
both being regulated on similar bases. A comparison between the home and colonial markets as
consumers of British produce, has been made with
remarkable ingenuity by Dr. Watson, with results
for which few persons will be prepared. For they
show that Australia in particular actually con-
sumes a larger quantity of English manufactures
in proportion to population than England herself.
In textile fabrics especially, while the English

consumption amounts to 2*l*. per head, the Australian consumption amounts to 3*l*. 4*s*. per head, the
difference being chiefly attributable to the easier
circumstances of the bulk of the Australian people.

But it is especially with reference to the future
prosperity of the mother country, and the maintenance of the rate of progress which we have thus
far attained, that Dr. Watson urges upon our
notice the importance of the colonies.

The paramount difficulty which has to be over-
come, is found in the growing dependence of the
United Kingdom upon external supplies of food.
Between 1869 and 1876, the value of the import
of food rose from 106,000,000*l*. to 159,000,000*l*.,
or at the rate of 50 per cent. ; the increase of
population in the same time being from 31,000,000
in 1869 to 33,000,000 in 1876, or only 6 per cent.
The normal annual increase in the demand for an
external supply of food is estimated at 6,000,000*l*. ;
while the progress in the exports of the net proceeds
of British industry is estimated at only 3,000,000*l*.,
or one-half of the sum required to keep up the
rates of exports and imports. The remedy is
anticipated in deriving our food supplies from the
British colonies, and so giving them the power to
increase our colonial exports. This also points to
the increase of colonial investments and systematic
emigration ; the first, as offering much greater
security than foreign countries, besides strength-
ening the ties between the different parts of the

same monarchy; while the second provides profitable employment to those who emigrate, and enlarged markets to those who stay at home.

To restore the balance of trade, and to derive our food supplies mainly from our own soil and our own people, is no doubt a great advantage to be gained on our side from extending to Englishmen on English soil abroad the same rights as Englishmen enjoy on English soil at home. On the other hand, to be placed in the same relation to English capitalists as inhabitants of the mother country; to be part and parcel of the monarchy, with an equal voice in all legislature that relates to the whole commonwealth; with a full share in the regulation and patronage of the public services, military, naval, diplomatic, and consular; in honours, dignities, and rewards; in the government of foreign, home, and intercolonial trade; in postal and telegraphic communication; and in every question affecting the whole nationality;—will be the satisfaction of a natural, hereditary, and loyal claim that the best exponents of colonial opinion have for a long time advocated.

IV.

ON HOME AND COLONIAL DEFENCE.

After the consideration of colonial trade from our own point of view, we might be expected to proceed to consider the same subject under the aspects which it presents to the colonies. But the subject of colonial defence absorbs that and all minor considerations. For it may be assumed that if any of the British colonies fell under a foreign flag, its trade and internal organization would have to bend to the will of the conqueror, and would be made subordinate to the interests of the paramount state.

In discussing the welfare of the mother country and her colonies, it must always be borne in mind that neither they nor the rest of the world are standing still. Vast political changes are taking place from day to day, among which the rise of such powers as the German Empire and the Kingdom of Italy may hereafter take quite a secondary place. The shores of the Atlantic and Indian Oceans and their great connected seas have hitherto held the chief place in the world's rivalry. At length, however, an active ferment has begun to work among the shores and islands of the vast expanse of the Pacific Ocean. Our Australian and American colonies and Asiatic settlements on the Pacific are acquiring a degree of wealth and importance which cannot fail to invite attack from our enemies in future naval wars. And in any forecast of a warlike nature we cannot be blind to the rapid strides which Russia has already made on the Pacific, or to the arsenals, dockyards, and fleets which she has formed on her shores. These war establishments have nothing to protect; for

defence all these preparations are wholly unre-
quired ; it is then expressly for offensive purposes
that these costly works have been made.

It is also necessary to note the extraordinary
growth of Japan in adopting European ideas and
modern armaments. Then, also, the vast and
numerically unequalled population of China is at
length entering on a similar career. With the
resources of one-third of the total population of
the whole earth, China is now forming her own
dockyards, and aiming at the establishment of a
navy after European models. Who can foresee
the coming effects of this awakening? The mi-
gration of the Chinese to the Pacific shores of
the United States, of Australia, and indeed of all
the European settlements on that great ocean, has
begun to be a matter of grave anxiety to the
Europeans, who are subject to their competition
and objectionable ways.

Another great power on the Pacific claims
attention, for it would not fail to be observed if
the United States of America were omitted from
this brief review, considering their great military
and naval prowess and exceeding commercial
activity. But one cannot name the people of the
United States, sprung mainly from our own Old
England, and as a nation adhering firmly to our
English tongue—one cannot speak of them as among
the possible foes in the future of their elder and
younger brethren. The idea is abhorrent to our

common origin, and we may be permitted to hope that, if ever conflict in the Pacific arises, the United States, if not with us, will be neutral. There are still other states in the Pacific which already possess ironclads, namely the republics of Spanish origin in Central and South America. These will have to be dealt with in future complications.

Our own interests in the Pacific are found in the Australian colonies of New South Wales, Queensland, Victoria, South Australia, and Western Australia; in Tasmania and New Zealand ; in the Fiji Islands ; in British Columbia and Vancouver, now nominally united, but still waiting to be welded by common interest and a continental railway, to Canada ; in Hong Kong, Labuan, and Singapore; besides our establishments in Japan and China, and our home and colonial shipping everywhere.

The true seats of British power in the Pacific are the coalfields and their ports in Vancouver Island, New Zealand, and New South Wales. The possession of these coalfields and their harbours in such commanding situations in the North and South Pacific respectively, and on opposite shores, must be the main reliance of the British fleet in that ocean for the fuel without which their activity must cease and their power be nullified. The absolute security of those colonial possessions is then not merely a matter of local or colonial concern, but one on which largely depends the maintenance of British

steam fleets, and the protection of British and
colonial commerce on these open seas.

On passing to the Indian Ocean, a glance reveals
the importance of combining in one, British and
colonial interests on those waters. The Indian
Empire, flanked by the two great British colonies,
South Africa on the one hand and Australia on
the other, would no longer be so dependent on
Great Britain, but would find in those neighbouring English settlements, after the contemplated
union, growing populations equally concerned with
ourselves in the possession of India. These addi-
tions to the recruiting grounds and military
resources of the British monarchy would constitute an ample counterpoise to the advance of the
threatening Russian flag up to the Oxus, the defined
limit of Russian sway towards India and Indian
waters.

In another direction, the Indian Ocean presents
on the east coast of Africa the most promising
avenues for the advancement of British trade and
civilization into the interior of that neglected but
rich and productive continent. It seems highly
probable that African enterprise would receive a
great impulse from an amalgamation of British and
colonial energy.

South Africa, besides being a portal of the Indian
Ocean, also guards the eastern entrance to the
Atlantic; while the Falkland Islands keep watch
and ward over the western approach round Cape

Horn and the Straits of Magellan. These, with
Tristan d'Acunha, St. Helena, and Ascension, far
apart in mid-ocean, are our only possessions on the
South Atlantic. On the African shores, north of the
equator, are the British settlements at Lagos and
the Gold Coast, at Sierra Leone, and at the Gambia,
still awaiting the enterprise which will hereafter
open to their trade the populous interior of the
Soudan, which stretches in a broad and fertile belt,
with numerous towns and villages, across the widest
part of the African continent, from the Atlantic to
the Nile and Abyssinia.

It is on the other side of the North Atlantic that
the oldest of our colonial possessions are distributed.
Newfoundland, still distinct from the Dominion of
Canada, is the nearest to the mother country of
our American territories. The Dominion of Canada
covers a vast tract of the continent along the
northern border of the United States, from the
Atlantic to the Pacific, with the navigable waters
facilitating communication and settlement between
the two oceans. The crying want of this vast
domain is the extension of the Canadian railway
system up to the coalfields of British Columbia and
Vancouver. The want of energy from the absence
of union between the mother country and Canada
is remarkably displayed in the railway connection
of the Atlantic and Pacific through the far more
different and objectionable ground along which it

has been carried in the United States, while the superior facilities of a Canadian line remain neglected and obstructed by divided interests. We must hope that this great want will not be brought home to us by some sad national disaster.

In the midst of the North Atlantic, about midway between Nova Scotia and the West Indies, and facing the shores of the United States, at a distance of about 800 miles, lies the British dockyard and arsenal of Bermuda. The British West India Islands, with British Guiana and Belize on the mainland, complete the series on this side of the Ocean, while Gibraltar, Malta, and now Cyprus, in the Mediterranean—the Channel Islands and Heligoland in the North Sea, off the Elbe—bring this part of our rapid story to its end.

The possession of these vast dominions, accessible, attractive, and in all parts of the world, is a consequence of our national prosperity, and a reward of our maritime enterprise; the colonies, indeed, being so many national landed estates added to the homes of all our countrymen, and open to the easy acquirement of any of us who are willing and able to replenish the earth and fulfil it. The colonies are like new lands recovered by Britons from the sea, and made part and parcel of the British Isles.

The defence of the whole of the British territories has hitherto been maintained by the mother country; but various circumstances have at length reached a point which demands common concurrence and united action in all matters of common interest, to the extent at least of those parts of the monarchy which have been entrusted by the Crown with parliamentary institutions.

The flourishing state of the colonies would undoubtedly expose them *especially* to attack in time of war. Their own resources would be insufficient for their defence against any great power. Their security lies in their acquisition of a right to claim a part in the defensive resources of the monarchy. On the other hand, the security of the mother country, and the effective use of the national armaments for the protection of all parts of her trade, territories, and communications, have become much modified since former naval wars—by steam power—by increasing dependence on external supplies of food—by the rapid growth of the colonies in population and wealth. Telegraphic communication has reduced distance to a minimum. The development of foreign docks, arsenals, and fleets, beyond the great headlands of the Atlantic, renders Old England no longer a sufficient base for naval operations beyond Cape Horn and the Cape of Good Hope. She now requires in the Young England at the Antipodes a new base, with complete resources, to fulfil the claims of world-wide responsibilities, and prevent the consequences that might follow from even the most temporary interruption of communications with the Southern Seas.

In the admirable papers read before the Royal Colonial Institute in 1873 and 1877, and before the Royal United Service Institution in 1879, Captain J. C. R. Colomb, R.M.A., has applied his professional science to the subjects of colonial defence and imperial and colonial responsibilities in war.* His papers have received the highest official commendation from the military authorities. He regards the main question to be—How to secure the imperial safety (that is, the safety of the whole monarchy) truly, efficiently, and economically. He exposes the fallacies which spring from merely local considerations, whether home or colonial. He teaches that a colony is indefensible if the rest of the monarchy be subjected; and that the defence of the monarchy includes the colonies and possessions of the Crown, as well as the defence of the United Kingdom. The indiscriminate formation of local forces tied to their own ground *must* be productive of general weakness instead of general strength. The United Kingdom, says Captain Colomb, is the military base of the whole monarchy, and for that reason must be secured, not only against capture, but also against the obstruction of its communications. If its communications were cut near home, the

* Lately issued in one volume, entitled 'The Defence of Great and Greater Britain.' Stanford, Charing Cross.

United Kingdom would become not only helpless itself, but it would cease to be a protection for the rest of the monarchy. Partial investment, even, would be of serious consequence to those parts cut off from their base or chief citadel. Thus, an enemy's fleet commanding the 1500 miles of sea between Cape St. Roque in South America, and Sierra Leone in Africa, while at the same time an obstruction was made in the Suez Canal, would stop all communications round Cape Horn and the Cape of Good Hope, and by the Red Sea.

The only security for all alike is in the military stronghold of commanding points provided with stores, coal, and repairing yards, for the support of naval supremacy over the lines of communication connecting those points.

The great lines of communication, with their strongholds, are as follows :—

1. The sea track to Canada; with Halifax, in Nova Scotia, at its western extremity.

2. The West Indies route; with defences at Bermuda, the Bahamas, Jamaica, and Antigua.

3. The India, Australasia, and China route by the Suez Canal; with defences at Gibraltar, Malta, Cyprus, Aden, Bombay, and Cape Comorin or Colachal. For the Australian branch of this route, King George's Sound, in Western Australia, is essential as a stronghold and coaling station; while for the China and Japan branch route,

Trincomalee, Singapore, and Hong Kong are required.

4. The Cape of Good Hope route. On this line Sierra Leone, Ascension, St. Helena, Simon's Bay, and Mauritius must be secured.

5. The Cape Horn and Pacific Ocean routes require the Falkland Isles, Fiji, Sydney, and Vancouver, to be proof against attack.

The paramount necessity of commanding and protecting the great sea routes is undeniably illus-trated by Captain Colomb from the exploits of the 'Alabama' and 'Sumter,' for which we paid so heavily. The necessity for protected coaling stations, under our sole control, is also displayed by the experience of the 'Alabama,' showing how their situation regulates and limits the operations of steam vessels and steam fleets. Steam commu-nication and steam fleets are comparatively inde-pendent of wind and weather, but they cannot move efficiently without fuel. Hence coaling stations determine the limits of the operations of modern fleets. The seizure of a coaling station by an enemy, would be tantamount to the dis-armament of any steam fleet that vainly depended on it for supplies. Then again, the destruction of the 'Alabama' illustrates the necessity for a naval repairing yard in the South Seas; for the want of one there, compelled her to resort to a European port, from which escape was made impossible.

The strategical points alluded to are generally said to be utterly neglected by Her Majesty's Government, and it is therefore urged that the colonies should unite in forcing attention to the subject through the Home and Colonial Parliaments.

Captain Colomb also insists on the following views :—

1. That the just relations between the colonies and the mother country in regard to common defence should be investigated and settled.

2. That the proper combination of the military and naval forces requires that the War Minister should overrule and connect the operations of the Admiralty with the Horse Guards, so as to secure the proper combination of the naval and military forces.

Colonial criticism on Captain Colomb's arguments indicates a disposition to expect that the defence of the communications across the seas should be provided wholly by the mother country, while each colony should be left to protect its own territory. But it is clearly proved by Captain Colomb that the command and security of certain colonial strongholds—as being no less essential to naval efficiency than our dockyards and arsenals at home—must be under the same control; and that colonial protection must be regarded not as a local matter but as a whole, because loss at any point is a weakness for all, and all resources

number of members in each House on the existing
scale, and a scale of one-third also, would be as
follows :—

Present Scale.			One-third Scale.	
Lords.	Commons.		Lords.	Commons.
435	493	England	145	164
16	60	Scotland	6	20
28	105	Ireland	10	35
15	75	Canada	5	25
1	3	Newfoundland	1	2
2	10	South Africa	2	4
2	10	New South Wales..	2	4
3	15	Victoria..	2	5
1	3	Queensland	1	2
1	4	South Australia	1	2
1	3	Tasmania	1	2
1	5	New Zealand..	1	2

The smaller scale seems quite ample for all purposes, while the larger makes an unnecessary
demand upon the most eminent and leading men
of the colonies. Thirty representatives from Canada
is a goodly number, and a sufficient strain upon its
population, while ninety would probably be felt as
excessive and burdensome. The limitation of the
English peerage in the Supreme Parliament, to a
selection of one-third of their number, bears a very
liberal aspect in comparison with their own treatment of the Scotch and Irish nobility, which, however justifiable, confined the complete exercise of
parliamentary privileges to 28 out of 183 peers of
Ireland, and to 16 out of 87 peers of Scotland.
This sacrifice of privilege has, however, been considerably qualified by the grant of peerages of the

E

United Kingdom to many of the Scotch and Irish nobles.

While the representatives of England, Ireland, and Scotland in the new Upper House would be elected by the peers of those kingdoms, the colonies would send to that Chamber, commoners of the same status as those who are now elected to the Upper House of their own local legislatures. All the elections to the Upper House should be for life, and probably the Crown would be persuaded to grant life peerages to life members from the colonies, besides creating hereditary baronies on the basis of colonial estates.

The election of the new Lower House on the larger scale would doubtless take place through the existing constituencies, but on the smaller scale some other arrangements would have to be made, which must be left to the wisdom of Parliament.

VI.

HOME AND COLONIAL DEFENCE.

In advocating the grand union of all the British people in a General Supreme Parliament, it is of prime importance that it should be seen that a general system of national defence can be made common to all parts of the monarchy alike, protecting all shores, ocean highways, home and colonial commerce and shipping, alike. Hence the

Royal navy and marines, besides being obviously the first line of defence against maritime attacks, and the instrument for crushing hostile fleets, would have the appointment of its officers by the Crown through an Admiralty under the influence of the Supreme Parliament in which the colonies would be fully represented. The manning of the navy would also be derived from the British colonies as well as from the British Isles. Thus the aspirations of Judge Haliburton would be realized, and a British ship-of-war in a colonial port should be as much entitled to feel itself at home there, as at any port in the C hannel.

Captain Colomb has demonstrated that the operations of steam fleets depend upon well distributed and protected coaling stations, and we ask whether all naval stations, including their garrisons and ports, should not be garrisoned entirely by the *Royal Marines*, so as to be thoroughly under one control, that of the Admiralty? The marines already include infantry and artillery of the very highest reputation, why should not their scientific qualifications be completed by adding a corps of marine engineers to them, for all fortresses connected with naval works?

The next point to be considered in this branch of our subject is the proper second line of defence for maritime countries. The navy sweeps the seas, and keeps them clear of hostile fleets. But in the event of accident or of circumstances which enable

an enemy to threaten a landing, what then ? To
meet this contingency something more than an
army is wanted. An army would doubtless be
the only fitting force to fight a battle of Dorking ;
but our spirit would be unlike that of our forefathers if we should even dream of letting an enemy
land. When the Spanish Armada threatened Old
England, the vast war-ships of Spain were encoun-
tered by every smack and lugger and coasting
vessel that could carry armed men. They swarmed
about the huge war-ships of the enemy, keeping
to the windward of them by *superior seamanship*,
which it must ever be our national aim to possess,
and, watching every opportunity, dealt many a
deadly blow. And so at length, with the elements
favouring our cause, the mighty invader became a
shattered and scattered wreck. And now, to-day,
the same spirit and the same course of action must
be followed equally at home and in our maritime
colonies.

The basis of a second line of maritime defence,
to keep an enemy from landing and to attack him
on the sea if he threatens the attempt, is to be
found, in the British Islands, in our coast-guard
stations and service. By this means already every
inch of the coast, with every creek and cranny
where a boat can land, is patrolled night and day,
and the sea, up to the bounding horizon, is kept
under watch and ward. Upon this professional
foundation should be built up a volunteer system,

not of soldiery, but of sailor-marines. The coast-guard stations, or a selection of them, could be readily adapted to serve the additional purpose of depôts for training volunteers from the surrounding gentry, farmers, villagers, and fishermen. These volunteers should be trained as marines to serve ashore or afloat, in batteries and in gun-boats, torpedo-boats, or any kind of craft that can be devised to float an effective weapon. We may rely upon the patriotism, liberality, ingenuity, and public spirit of our country gentry, farmers, and rural population to provide in this effective manner for their own local defence. Abundant scope would thus be given for invention and ingenuity in naval weapons. We all know what a charm and attraction there is in the sea and boating to the youth of the country; and we may be sure that the whole country side within reach of the shore, would fall in with a system of volunteering which made them adepts in boating and seaman-ship, as well as in gunnery and shooting. Many a country gentleman would prefer his volunteer, well-manned gunboat or cutter, launch or lugger, to infantry or yeomanry exercise; and it is ob-vious that an immense auxiliary force would thus be available in support of the coast-guard. The leisure hours of our rural population would thus be turned to account, not only in the defence of their own homes against some future " Paul Jones," or grand armada, but also in qualifying

the surplus of them for the manning of our mer-
chantmen and the Royal navy, for which we are
now too dependent on the population of the great
maritime towns.

The principle of such a measure has been adopted
by the Admiralty and the Legislature in the Act
for the establishment of the Royal Naval Volunteer
Artillery. But the operation of that Act has been
too much confined to large ports, so that it has
failed to become a popular movement. Moreover,
too little is to be seen by the public of what is done,
and thus it fails to be attractive. Whereas, by the
combination of land and water drills, and the am-
phibious qualifications of the Royal Marines, which
render them in a most especial manner a popular
and exceedingly effective corps, we should unite all
that would help to make an attractive service, and
one of great value to the State in many important
respects. Coasts thus guarded would be treated
with respect by enemies of all kinds, especially by
privateers, who have in former wars landed with
impunity, carried off much plunder, and caused
great destruction to private property. It will be
obvious that such a method is applicable to every
coast where habitations and wealth attract hostility,
and where the population can be trained for its own
defence, at the same time becoming qualified for
maritime pursuits.   •

By the general adoption of this second line of
defence, the Militia and Military Volunteers, under

qualified officers, would constitute a movable force for the defence of fortresses and the support of the second line wherever it may be especially threatened. The Regular Army, with its high training and discipline, would thus be at the disposal of the State wherever its services were required. It should be, like the navy, regarded as a purely *Offensive* arm, the *burden of Defence* being thrown upon the local forces, formed by the Coast Guard, Yeomanry, Militia, and Military Volunteers.

It may appear that this subject of national defence has received too much prominence as a part of the question of the union of the colonies with the mother country. But, in fact, *community of defence* is the touchstone of all independent nationality; and the practicability of providing for it from a common fund, gives occasion for the civil organization which in free countries manages the levying and expenditure of that and other common funds subordinate to it. The civil organization best adapted to unite the colonies and mother country under one fold and one shepherd, requires a system of parliamentary representation coupled with responsible ministries on a basis common to all the distinct yet conjoint parliamentary divisions of the monarchy; and for this object in particular, it is necessary to withdraw imperial and general affairs from the present Houses of the British Parliament and from the Executive of the United Kingdom, and to transfer

them to a newly constituted and distinct Supreme
Parliament and Executive for such affairs especially,
in which the United Kingdom and the nine parliamentary colonies shall be proportionably represented.

LONDON : PRINTED BY EDWARD STANFORD, 55, CHARING CROSS. S.W.

TATIVE LEGISLATURE, AND A RESPONSIBLE MINISTRY.

Population.	Revenue.	Public Debt.	
		Colonial Office List.	Statistical Abstracts for Colonies by Board of Trade
3,670,577	£4,474,002	£34,991,463	£27,751,812
161,374	212,293	151,742	275,136
720,984	1,586,303	9,344,590	5,024,959
712,019	6,708,047	14,973,519	11,721,419
210,510	1,559,111	10,192,150	7,865,350
878,243	4,991,919	20,048,222	17,018,913
248,795	1,592,634	6,622,500	4,737,200
107,104	386,060	1,788,560	1,589,705
432,519	3,551,783	23,222,311	20,691,111

LEGISLATURE AND CROWN EXECUTIVES.

by the Crown with an Elected Assembly.

43,000	41,518	77,280	61,162
162,042	139,131	—	25,130
12,121	26,903	11,484	11,484

ber, partly Appointed, and partly Elected.

152,653	189,536	Not stated.	
120,499	96,273	50,262	74,411
37,684	34,078	10,000	7,000
17,054	14,306	None.	
232,636	409,259	27,000	323,563
356,617	369,383	1,631,700	1,231,700
28,166	163,314	None.	
50,000	105,727	250,000	—

rernor and Crown Council under Statutes.

506,154	513,465	741,644	633,435
24,710	41,417	—	5,041
35,688	28,483	None.	
1,415	3,838	None.	
14,190	26,546	None.	
37,039	63,125	66,000	—
454,051	154,480	—	Lagos 288
307,951	366,447	100,000	—

and Crown Council.

109,638	470,513	278,000	178,000
35,474	28,297	39,700	44,100
800,000	79,962	260,000	260,000
354,623	789,544	800,000	1,000,000
2,401,066	1,543,320	1,375,000	773,812
4,893	7,418	None.	
139,144	197,424	None.	
121,600	61,021	None.	

r alone makes Laws.

1,912	7,475	1,871	—
18,014	41,161	None.	
6,241	14,197	12,250	—

der the Home Secretary.

90,596	—	—	—
54,042	...	—	—

Admiralty.

400	—	—	—

State for India in Council.

40,937,315	58,969,301	146,684,770	—

Quebec, New Brunswick, Nova Scotia, Prince Edward Island, British Columbia,

Grenada, Tobago, St. Lucia, each under Lieutenant-Governors. The Governor of

n), St. Christopher (n), with Anguilla (c), Nevis (n), Dominica (c), Virgin (n), and
Nominated Council.
¶ Transvaal has a Nominee Assembly besides the Council.
Council), the Chagos Islands, including Diego Garcia.
n subordinate governments, under which all the British and Native administrations
Bengal, but not Aden and Perim, which are also British, and under the Government
direct correspondence with the Secretary of State for India.

ut which, having no resident British officials, are usually omitted in
rgia, &c., in the South Atlantic ; Socotra, Kuria-Muria, &c., in the
e Southern Ocean.
List and from the Statistical Abstract for the Colonies issued by the

British Possessions under the Colonial Secretary of State.

I.—COLONIES WITH A CROWN GOVERNOR, REPRESENTATIVE LEGISLATURE, AND A RESPONSIBLE MINISTRY.

	Area in Square Miles.	Population.	Revenue.	Public Debt.	
				Colonial Office List.	Statistical Abstract for Colonies by Board of Trade
Canada * (America)	3,400,542	3,670,077	£4,474,962	£34,901,463	£27,161,912
Newfoundland (America)	40,200	181,374	213,293	161,742	275,126
Cape Colony (South Africa)	223,204	720,984	1,686,302	8,344,890	6,074,959
New South Wales and Norfolk Island (Australia)..	323,000	712,019	6,700,017	14,873,619	11,724,419
Queensland (Australia)	668,420	216,610	1,863,111	10,192,150	7,865,350
Victoria ,, ...	86,944	876,313	4,993,910	20,064,272	17,014,913
South Australia ,, ...	906,900	248,795	1,592,634	5,623,600	4,177,220
Tasmania ,, ...	26,205	107,104	366,060	1,779,500	1,509,705
New Zealand ,, ...	105,000	472,319	3,651,743	23,972,311	26,691,111

II.—COLONIES WITH A REPRESENTATIVE LEGISLATURE AND CROWN EXECUTIVES.

1. Crown Governor and Council appointed by the Crown with an Elected Assembly.

Bahama Islands † (West Indies),..	2,921	43,000	41,616	77,290	91,162
Barbados, Windward Islands ‡ (West Indies).. ..	166	163,042	139,131	—	26,130
Bermuda Islands (North Atlantic)	19½	13,121	26,903	11,481	11,481

2. Crown Governor and Legislative Chamber, partly Appointed, partly Elected.

Malta and Gozo (Europe)	143	192,653	148,536	Not stated.	
Leeward Islands § (West Indies)	659	120,190	96,373	56,363	74,411
Grenada, Windward Islands ‡ (West Indies)	133	37,844	34,978	16,900	7,000
Tobago, Windward Islands ‡	114	17,054	14,306	None.	
British Guiana (South America)	76,000	232,638	409,259	27,000	323,863
Natal (South Africa)	21,000	356,817	363,363	1,031,700	1,231,700
Western Australia	1,060,000	29,166	163,311	None.	—
Griqua Land West (South Africa)	17,800	50,000	105,127	256,000	—

III.—CROWN COLONIES. 1. Crown Governor and Crown Council under Statutes.

Jamaica, with Turks Islands, and Caicos Islands (West Indies)	4,200	506,154	513,465	741,814	633,435
British Honduras (Central America)	7,562	24,710	41,411	—	8,041
St. Vincent, Windward Islands ‡ (West Indies) ..	171	35,688	24,475	None.	
Falkland Islands (South Atlantic)	6,500	1,415	3,834	None.	
Gambia (West Africa)	20	14,190	26,546	None.	
Sierra Leone	468	37,089	63,125	68,000	—
Gold Coast and Lagos (West Africa)	15,286	484,361	184,490	—	Lagos 234
Straits Settlements ‖ (Asia)	1,446	307,351	366,447	100,850	—

2. Crown Governor and Crown Council.

Trinidad (West Indies)	1,754	109,079	478,513	278,000	178,000
St. Lucia, Windward Islands ‡ (West Indies)	237	35,474	38,257	39,700	44,100
Transvaal ¶ (South Africa)	114,000	800,000	79,963	260,000	260,000
Mauritius ** (Indian Ocean)	713	314,023	748,544	800,800	1,000,000
Ceylon ,, ...	24,700	2,481,206	1,643,320	7,375,000	773,433
Labuan (China Sea)	30	4,894	7,414	None.	
Hong Kong ,, ...	32	139,344	187,424	None.	
Fiji Islands (Pacific Ocean)	7,403	131,600	61,021	None.	

3. Crown Governor alone makes Laws.

Heligoland (North Sea)..	¼	1,912	7,476	1,871	—
Gibraltar (Mediterranean)	2	18,604	41,181	None.	
St. Helena (South Atlantic)	46	5,241	14,197	12,250	—

British Possessions under the Home Secretary.

Channel Islands (English Channel)	75	90,556	—	—	—
Isle of Man (Irish Sea)	227	54,042	—	—	—

Under the Admiralty.

Ascension Island (South Atlantic)	35	400	—	—	—

Under the Secretary of State for India in Council.

India †† (Asia)	1,475,876	240,237,815	54,969,301	146,641,770	—

* Canada, including eight provinces with Local Governments, viz. Ontario, Quebec, New Brunswick, Nova Scotia, Prince Edward Island, British Columbia, Manitoba, and North-West Territory, also Arctic Lands and Hudson Bay.
† Bahama include twenty inhabited islands.
‡ Windward Islands include Barbados, under a Governor, and St. Vincent, Grenada, Tobago, St. Lucia, each under Lieutenant-Governors. The Governor of Barbados is also Governor-in-chief of the whole of the islands.
§ Leeward Islands include the six presidencies of Antigua (c), Montserrat (a), St. Christopher (a), with Anguilla (c), Nevis (a), Dominica (c), Virgin (a), and their dependent islands united as one colony. Note.—(c) Crownpalm Council. (a) Nominated Council.
‖ Straits Settlements include Singapore, Penang, Wellesley, and Malacca. ¶ Transvaal has a Nominee Assembly besides the Council.
** Mauritius has the following dependencies:—Rodrigues, Seychelles (Nominee Council), the Chagos Islands, including Diego Garcia.
†† India is under the general government of the Viceroy in Council, with fifteen subordinate governments, under which all the British and Native administrations are administered. These include the Andaman and Nicobar Islands in the Bay of Bengal, but not Aden and Perim, which are also British, and under the Government of India. Besides the Viceroy, only the Governors of Madras and Bombay are in direct correspondence with the Secretary of State for India.

. There are other islands to which England lays claims; but which, having no resident British officials, are usually omitted in printed papers. Among such are Tristan d'Acunha, South Georgia, &c., in the South Atlantic: Socotra, Kuria-Muria, &c., in the Indian Ocean; Pitcairn, &c., in the Pacific; and many more in the Southern Ocean.

The Public Debts are quoted both from the Colonial Office List and from the Statistical Abstract for the Colonies issued by the Board of Trade, because of the discrepancies between the two.